I Count is the campaign of Stop Climate Chaos, a coalition of more than 30 organisations with over 700 years' combined experience of making the impossible possible. Together we are millions of people - *and counting*.

icount.org.uk

PENGUIN BOOKS

Published by the Penguin Group
Penguin Books Ltd, 80 Strand, London WC2R ORL, England
Penguin Group (USA) Inc., 375 Hudson Street, New York, New York 10014, USA
Penguin Group (Canada), 90 Eglinton Avenue East, Suite 700, Toronto, Ontario, Canada M4P 2Y3
(a division of Pearson Penguin Canada Inc.)
Penguin Ireland, 25 St Stephen's Green, Dublin 2, Ireland (a division of Penguin Books Ltd)
Penguin Group (Australia), 250 Camberwell Road, Camberwell, Victoria 3124, Australia
(a division of Pearson Australia Group Pty Ltd)
Penguin Books India Pvt Ltd, 11 Community Centre, Panchsheel Park, New Delhi – 110 017, India
Penguin Group (NZ), 67 Apollo Drive, Rosedale, North Shore 0632, New Zealand
(a division of Pearson New Zealand Ltd)
Penguin Books (South Africa) (Pty) Ltd, 24 Sturdee Avenue, Rosebank, Johannesburg 2196, South Africa

Penguin Books Ltd, Registered Offices: 80 Strand, London WC2R ORL, England

www.penguin.com

First published 2006
4

Copyright © Stop Climate Chaos, 2006
All rights reserved

Printed in England by Clays Ltd, St Ives plc

ISBN: 978-0-141-03025-8

Written by Rob Alcraft
Designed by Provokateur
Illustrated by James Joyce
Special thanks to Matthew Davis

Stop Climate Change is the operating name of
The Climate Movement, registered charity number 1109973

www.greenpenguin.co.uk

Penguin Books is committed to a sustainable future
for our business, our readers and our planet.
The book in your hands is made from paper
certified by the Forest Stewardship Council.

I Count

Together we can stop climate chaos

Your step-by-step guide to climate bliss.

We **can** stop climate chaos

You are irresistible

Admit it. You feel it too.

You are irresistible. *We* are irresistible. With small steps we can do almost anything we choose.

Just as we have polluted our world to the point of climate chaos, we also have the resources and the knowledge to save it. It comes down to what we want, what we dream of. If we choose, we can make our politicians take the action needed. They cannot resist us all. We can stop climate chaos.

We only have to start. This book is about how.

 There are **16 no-nonsense steps**, and with each one you will find a new level of happiness – shall we begin?

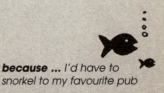

because ... I'd have to snorkel to my favourite pub

Make it count

We are living through a disordered upward slide in temperatures unique in 800,000 years. Within our lifetimes we face climate chaos – unless we do something to stop it.

>> Step 1

First thing we have to do is locate which part of your brain is working today. Use this mood tester to find out.

happy

confused

dreamy

determined

1. You find twenty quid in a coat you haven't worn for a year. Do you:

a) treat your friend to a slap-up curry?

b) set light to it and dance round shouting 'I don't believe in climate change'?

c) buy a tree to give a friend for their garden?

d) go and buy some really good low-polluting local food from a farmers' market?

2. A friend sees you reading this book and says, 'What's that about then?' Do you:

a) tell them?

b) bind the book tightly with rolls of tape so they can't take a look?

c) tell them they're irresistible?

d) go and buy them a copy, and point out the postcard at the back?

3. You spot a high profile politician on a train. Do you:

a) sit next to them and find out what they think about climate chaos?

b) lick the side of their face?

c) have a chat with them about their favourite places?

d) challenge them about their lifestyle and their record on voting climate friendly?

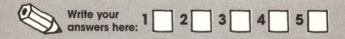

4. You quite like bonobo monkeys and your ex asks you to the zoo to see them. Do you:

a) go along for a laugh?

b) grip hold of your ex's buttocks and make alarming howling noises until you are eventually arrested?

c) invite them instead to watch gorillas on your new nature channel?

d) explain the need to protect wild habitat from climate change, and invite them on a conservation weekend instead?

5. While on holiday in South America you're offered a rare species of parrot for supper. Do you:

a) tuck in, but use the meal as a chance to talk about the endangered bird?

b) eat the entire bird and demand more endangered species be brought to you and roasted whole?

c) tuck in, because this is a poor family and it is a generous offer?

d) explain why you can't eat it, and that there's a local project which pays people to protect the birds?

How did you count?

Mostly a's: Good, you are in a people mood. Get involved and spread the word.

Mostly b's: You seem confused. This book will help clear your mind.

Mostly c's: You're feeling dreamy, and we like it. We need the power of dreams.

Mostly d's: You feel steely – you have excellent determination and single mindedness, let's get going.

We think you're ready. Let's start with the problem.

7

How did we get here and what will it mean?

The problem is carbon dioxide and other greenhouse gasses – we'll call them CARBON to keep things simple.

Forests that used to absorb carbon dioxide have been cleared for farming.

Think greenhouse.

By polluting our atmosphere we're trapping more of the sun's heat.

There's a serious risk of sea levels rising 10–90cm this century. Where did you say you used to live?

Glaciers are melting. Ice thickness over the Arctic is thought to have shrunk by up to 15%.

For a more complete science experience see the Intergovernmental Panel on Climate Change at **ipcc.ch**, also the UK Climate Impacts Programme at **ukcip.org.uk**.

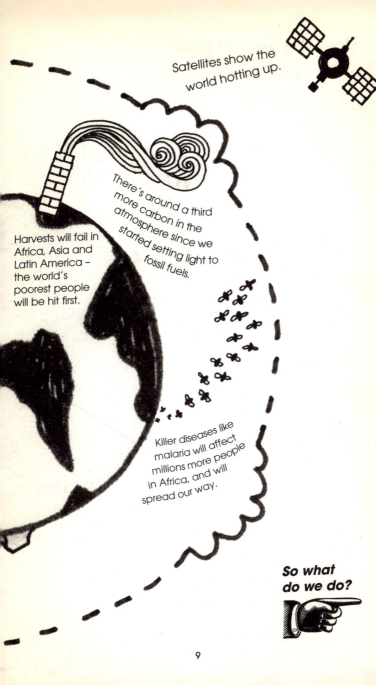

Satellites show the world hotting up.

There's around a third more carbon in the atmosphere since we started setting light to fossil fuels.

Harvests will fail in Africa, Asia and Latin America – the world's poorest people will be hit first.

Killer diseases like malaria will affect millions more people in Africa, and will spread our way.

So what do we do?

9

We're here

We in the UK puff and belch into the air almost 2 million tonnes of carbon every 24 hours. It's heading us to a possible rise in average global temperatures of up to 5.8°C by the end of this century – maybe even more. This will be climate chaos.

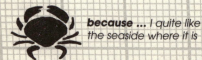

because ... I quite like the seaside where it is

We need to be here

Your carbon count:

◻ **4, 8 0 0** kg

aim to cut carbon to this

Each one of us must cut carbon –
but we can only do part of what's
needed. Government must do
the rest with at least 3% year-on-
year carbon cuts. If we act now
we can keep global temperature
rises to below 2°C – and stop
climate chaos.

Feel the power of off

You can do this. Feel the power; it is all around you. It is the power of off, and it is limitless.

Let us begin.

With one finger applied to a TV **off** button you could save 20kg-worth of carbon pollution in a single year. UK-wide that's nearly half a million tonnes of carbon. That's a poke in the eye for climate chaos, and all it takes is a finger. This is the power of off.

Off	Carbon saving	Cash saving this year
telly off standby	20kg	£3.70
stereo off standby	66kg	£12
dvd off standby	44kg	£8
computer off standby	9kg	£1.70
turn off lights you don't need	370kg	£55
unplug your mobile phone charger	10.5kg	£1.90
Carbon saved **Cash saved**	**519.5kg**	**£82.30**

You're ready. So go now.

The average house in this country has 12 items on standby. Hunt them down, turn them off, and don't worry, they'll remember what time it is. You can come back when you've finished.

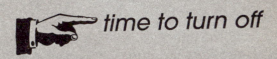 *time to turn off*

starting is everything

Fresh from your carbon kicking, you should know this: you have now saved, in a single giant step around the house, an amount of carbon pollution equivalent to that absorbed by **one good-sized tree**. You should now rest briefly.

  Consider this. If every person in the UK did what you just did, it would save the entire year's energy output, and carbon pollution, from **two old-style power stations**.

 OK, back on your feet. Are there other switches you may have missed?

because ... *2 billion people don't have 'leccy anyway*

*make **off** your new **on***

We **can** stop climate chaos

As well as off, there is **easy**.

Say off to the Prime Minister

Get worked up – there's your very own action card at the back to kick you off. The more we are the more the impact.

Dear Prime Minister

Buy cool

The next time an appliance of yours packs up, replace it with an A** rated one – look for the shop label that will tell all. Potential savings over your old appliance per year are up to £45 and around 200kg of carbon.

Use technology

Power use in the UK home has doubled since the 1970s. But using an old technology such as a washing line will save 1.5kg of carbon over its hi-tech drier equivalent. Saucepan lids work too – saving up to 90% on the heat you have to put into cooking. Impressive.

Win £100!

Fit one of these and over its lifetime you will save yourself £100 and around 60kg of carbon a year. OK, it's hardly clinging to Big Ben to make your point, but it works. In fact *if every UK household installed three energy-saving light bulbs the energy saved would supply all street lighting in the UK.*

Your carbon saving:
8 5 7. 5 kg
an excellent use of **off**

Master your
thermostat

It's time to take a quick peek at your habits. You see, though you are in general a deeply appealing kind of person, you still need a little gentle modification.

For this step you are going to acquire two new habits. Couldn't be easier. You may even feel a not unpleasant fizzing sensation.

1st

find your hot water thermostat.
When you get there turn it
down to 60°C. Done? Get this,
for every 1°C you've just saved
yourself an easy tenner and – for
a gas boiler – around 10kg of
carbon. Easy. Let's keep going.

2nd

**give your favourite person
a call** and invite them to
share your next warm bath –
or, even better, a nice efficient
shower. You can tell them
all about how much carbon
pollution you've avoided as
you splash about.

*because ...my 'it's hopeless'
feeling will start to lift*

HAPPINESS COUNTER

1 2 3 4 5 6 7 8 9 10

this is win-win

Let's not kid about.

Turning your heating down 1°C is not going to prevent the imminent wipe out of polar bears on its own (they won't live without the summer ice-flows threatened by climate chaos). But it's a start. And if all the households in the UK did the same thing, we'd save the kind of carbon you need more than 1.2 million trees to soak up. Pretty good, don't you think?

3 more things to do when you're naked

1

Call more friends and tell them how you've saved an easy tenner and done the kind of carbon-saving work it would take a good-sized tree nearly 3 weeks to achieve.

2

Email a politician – ask what they're doing about energy efficiency and climate chaos. You can find your MP, MSP or Assembly Member's name and email at **upmystreet.com**.

3

Draw an I Count tattoo on your bath buddy.

Respect your planet

Dear

You are cordially invited to share a bath with

at   p.m. Bring a towel.

 Find out more about energy efficient housing at **wwf.org.uk** and **foe.co.uk**. If polar bears are your thing see Greenpeace's **projectthinice.org**.

›› Step 4
Find a jumper you like.
Put it on

You're getting warmer

in case ... I come back as an arctic squirrel

OK, cover up. Easy this one, isn't it? Now you look good, and you feel good. You're warm.

This is why you should never underestimate the power of a jumper. Your torso-shaped woolly garment is going to help stop climate chaos.

So, with your jumper on, step towards the central heating thermostat. **You know the drill by now.** Steady, turn the dial down 1°C. Rest.

In an average winter your action will save around £30, and 250kg of carbon.

Good stuff.

you like your jumper and your jumper likes you

HAPPINESS COUNTER
1 2 3 4 5 6 7 8 9 10

23

Nothing funky to put on?

Call five friends about your size;
invite them – and their wardrobe
– around to yours. Get some
nibbles. Hey presto, party.

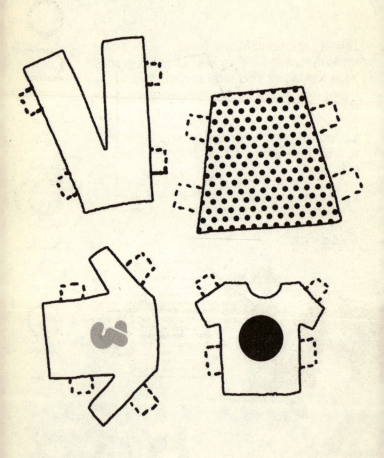

Don't be sad – swap.

So hot right now!

Love your fridge

Your fridge is your friend – but you may need to say goodbye. Nuzzle its little thermostat if you like, but if your fridge is more than 10 years old, it is costing you cash and causing carbon pollution.

You see, just as we've moved on from Space Invaders, so fridge technology has also advanced. In a single year a new A** rated fridge will save more than 140kg of carbon, and around £51.

Of course, you may be way too broke to fork out for a new fridge. In which case defrost your little friend regularly to keep it efficient, and when it finally dies, send it straight to recycling heaven via your council.

because ... cavity wall insulation would keep me warm

Love your fridge, but not too much.

 Now we've sorted the machine, let's have a poke around inside, shall we?

this might hurt
but it will make
you stronger

Oh my, we have to talk.

We'll start with that jet-set Californian lettuce. It takes more than 60 times the energy just getting it here than you'll get from eating it. In fact, one basketful of imported food creates more carbon than an average family's cooking for 6 months.

So don't let glowing, far-flung vegetables turn your head. Buy local food when you can, it causes less carbon. For the rest of your shopping buy fairtrade food - it comes a long way but it helps the kind of people who will lose most from climate chaos. Oh, and one last thing, try repeating the word allotment to yourself for a few days – see what happens.

 For more on food, fair trade and what you can do try Oxfam at **oxfam.org.uk**. **tearfund.org** is also hot on what's good to shop for from a long way off.

For information on food miles visit the New Economics Foundation at **nef.org.uk**.

If you're hungry and you want to know what to buy right now you'll find joy at your local farmers' market. People from around your way will sell you stuff they've grown or made themselves. A novel idea. More on this at **farmersmarkets.net**.

The WI is also a good source of home-produced goodies. Find out more at **womens-institute.co.uk**.

28

Feed me local food

We **can** stop climate chaos

January	leeks, kale, venison
February	carrots, onions, rabbit
March	purple sprouting broccoli, scallops, spring onions
April	watercress, potatoes, rhubarb, pigeon, wild salmon
May	asparagus, sorrel, radishes, brown crab
June	beetroot, peas, gooseberries, lamb, mackerel
July	broad beans, cucumber, strawberries, cherries, lobster
August	courgettes, french beans, hazelnuts, raspberries, blackberries,
September	sweetcorn, tomatoes, plums, goose
October	pumpkin, apples, chestnuts, eel
November	cauliflower, sprouts, pears, partridge, mussels
December	cabbage, artichoke, parsnip, pheasant

Get your regular seasonal food alerts at icount.org.uk/stepbystep

Face your elephant

In your lifetime you will drink around 75,000 cups of tea, eat 13,345 eggs and flush away 119.1 km of toilet paper.

While you're about it, you'll discard over 31,000 drinks cans and have hefted into waste sites around 5 television sets, 7 computers, and – possibly – 1 trampoline. You will drive more than 722,000 miles and spend 129 days ironing. Carbon-wise, you have impact.

HAPPINESS COUNTER

1 2 3 4 5 6 7 8 9 10

everyone loves
an elephant

30

This is your own personal carbon elephant, and you have to face it.

Look it in the eye, and take it one step at a time.

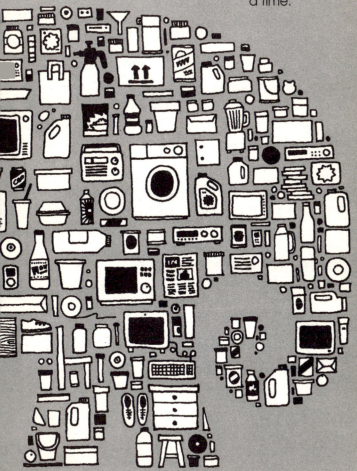

31

re-use

Some of the greatest vintage designer clothes ever bought have come from charity shops. And there are now enough auction sites to make your head spin. So flog things, and buy stuff second hand – this is good because the first rule of tackling your carbon elephant is re-use.

 re-use it, every bag saved is worth 62.5g carbon – that's around 25kg a year

 flog it

 take it to your favourite charity shop

 take your own coffee cup into town

 try freecycle.org, great for freebies, and a chance to give stuff away

don't buy daft things

You know deep down in your soul that you do not need a plastic bag to walk 3 metres to a shop door, or a sandwich box designed for a life of 30 seconds. Refuse stuff with crazy packaging.

 make your own lunch and save up to £1000 a year

reduce and repair

A typical AA rechargeable battery will in its sparky little life-time save you around £326 – and that includes buying a solar charger. Using washable nappies instead of disposables could save you up to £500 per baby. Don't buy stuff you're just going to chuck out.

 get it fixed

 every rechargeable battery can save £100s

recycle

You know you want to, and you know you can. It's time to revisit your understanding of the word 'bin'. Around 80% of what an average person in the UK chucks out can be happily recycled – which is a lot better than paying your council to put it in holes in the ground.

 sort your rubbish

 start a compost heap (allotment, allotment)

 for a complete product-by-product guide try **greenchoices.org/recycling**. *The Women's Environmental Network also has useful information at* **wen.org.uk**

 For more on door-to-door recycling visit Friends of the Earth at **foe.co.uk** – you can find out exactly what your council should be doing for you.

There are now other, larger carbon elephants we can face. But happily these are elephants we share.

We can face them together.

Dare

1

This is for your sociable mood.

Use the power of sharing, and have a climate chaos supper for friends. Use local food and hi-tech solutions like pan lids, and low energy lighting. Talk a little bit of climate chaos; there are some clever clog answers to use on **page 46**. As political actions go, a pretty pleasant evening.

Dare

2

Get to work on your work.

Paper recycling, thermostat turning, low energy bulbs – you name it, do it. If it's not happening, why not? And don't forget there's always the option of bringing in the professionals – see **page 38** for organising a full energy-saving treatment.

Visit a politician.

No, don't shuffle about: listen. This dare will multiply the impact of anything you're already doing, and your MP, MSP or Assembly Member will have an office local to you, so really – it's a doddle.

Make an appointment and use it to say what you've done to cut carbon, and then find out what they're doing. If you want advice before you go, visit us at **icount.org.uk/stepbystep**, details on **page 77**. Take a friend if you feel at all unsure, or drop them a line or an email.

Remember, you can find your local politician's name and email at **upmystreet.com**.

How are you saving?

Your carbon saving:
2, 1 1 4 .5 kg
recycle and reuse

Dump your
dinosaurs

**This one is
a liberation –
it's a skip.**

Combine this with your new extra-efficient lifestyle and the sun is really coming out. You're going to switch to green energy. You get to dump that smoky old power company that keeps sending you bills, and you prevent a whale-sized weight of carbon pollution.

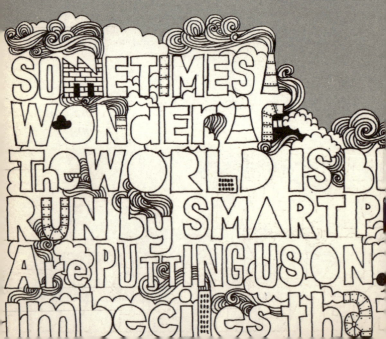

find joy in your
electricity bill

The beauty of it is that switching has never been easier.

No grim calls. No sobbing.

Just choose a renewable power company and sign up online. They even deliver the bad news to your ex-company for you. Of course, you still get a bill, but nothing's perfect is it?

Ready?

Go to **energylinx.co.uk/green electricity.htm** or **greenconsumerguide.com**. There'll be companies there you like, and you're a grown up, so choose one.

Of course, you old softie, you could give your current supplier one last chance. Call them; talk it through. Can they offer you a green deal?

One more thing

What about the places where you work, or study or meet? You could be the bright spark that helps them switch. And it's more than just electricity. Energy can be saved in so many ways, from pub to church, from mosque to office. Liberate them, and you will have real impact.

 For help with this go to carbontrust.co.uk/costs – these people offer a free energy audit, and practically guarantee to save a business or institution money. That should help.

Your carbon saving:
3, 8 0 8 kg
the dinosaur is gone

The big UK power companies chuck out around a third of all UK carbon pollution. A little consumer kicking will help convince them that **the time has come to invest in clean technologies.**

Make some juice

Anyway, who says we have to lock ourselves into another 50 years of inflexible central supply? We could have our own turbines, our own solar panels. Let's bring power to the people. We would see it made, so would use it with more care. The technology is already here. Feel that shiver coming down the wires.

We've got 40% of Europe's wind – have some

OK, it's not cheap, but there are government grants that will pay half your costs. And if you don't own your own home what about a community wind generator, or solar power for your office or kid's school? It's happening already: there's a farm in Wales, a school in Kirby. Where do you live, what could you do?

Have a look at these sites, and dream the dream.
lowcarbonbuildings.org.uk
est.org.uk

There's more than 10,000 times
as much solar energy falling
on the Earth than all our
other fuel use combined
– have your share

Take sides

This one's a toughie. You have to take sides.

On one side you do nothing. You live like you always have. This is the numb nut option, and it embraces climate chaos.

DO NOTHING

 because ... *I don't think I want to go extinct just yet*

On the other side you do the things you can, so that your carbon footprint on the Earth is as small as it can be.

DO SOMETHING

Do something

every recycled bottle is worth **=** 0.5kg
carbon saved

bike or walk short journeys and save **=** 2kg
carbon saved every journey under 3 miles that you walk and don't use the car

use the washing line not the drier and save **=** 1.5kg
carbon saved

don't forget the power of off **=** 30kg
carbon saved

work one day every week from home and you save **=** 880kg
carbon saved

switch your office to recycled paper and you could save **=** 2,300kg
carbon saved

Do nothing

every cup you boil is 25 cups more of carbon: just boil what you need

one year's driving **=** **5,000kg** carbon used

every time you chuck a bag of rubbish out it's **=** **20kg** carbon used

1kg of beef **=** **5kg** carbon equivalent used

one flight to Barcelona – going by rail would emit 95% less carbon **=** UK average **1,109kg** carbon used

 collective action on these kinds of things makes the most impact

 Find out more at
carboncalculator.org.uk
safeclimate.net/calculator/

45

>> Step 9
Answer back

For this step you need to get lippy. Summon up your steely side. Down the pub, in the office, with the family – don't give up, just answer back. Here's some ammo.

No one **actually knows for sure** that this climate chaos thing is happening, *do they?*

You say: Actually no one but an irritating bunch of oil-eating axe-grinding cranks is arguing about this any more – *even in the US.*

But don't take my word for it; the world authority on this is the Intergovernmental Panel on Climate Change – look 'em up. Hundreds of top scientists from around the world are involved. They're using the best scientific and technical information available. They say if we don't do something quick, by the end of this century there could be a global temperature rise of anything between 1.4°C and 5.8°C – and maybe even more.

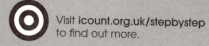

Visit icount.org.uk/stepbystep to find out more.

Anyway, **isn't the climate always changing**, like with ice ages and *woolly mammoths?*

You say: That's correct – there have been natural changes in climate. But what's different now is that *we* are making the climate change – and it's happening quicker than anything we know about from the past.

In fact we've filled our atmosphere with bigger concentrations of greenhouse gases than at any time in the last 800,000 years. So what's happening now is entirely new in the history of humans. Life for us could be about to get a whole lot harder.

The Hadley Centre will tell you more about this. Find them at **metoffice.com/research/hadleycentre**.

Great does this mean we get to have **a proper summer?**

You say: Look hoof-foot, you're not making sense. We won't be lying around on the beach. Our climate will get warmer and wetter, but we'll also get more extreme weather. That's what you'll need to worry about – and anyway, with sea levels rising, you'll need a lilo if you go anywhere near the beach.

To be serious for a moment, the real problem is going to be in the poorest places around the world, where people already live on the edge. This is where more extreme weather – such as drought – could make life impossible for millions of people.

 See **christian-aid.org.uk,** **cafod.org.uk, oxfam.org.uk, tearfund.org.uk** and **action aid.org.uk** for more on what climate chaos could mean for the world's poorest people.

So **I have to wear your old pants** and live in the dark do I? *I think I'd rather fry.*

You say: You can wear my old pants if you want,

but it would be better to make the kind of fairly painless and sensible changes to the way you live described in a rather pertinent little book I've just read.

And overall as a country, I admit it, the changes we need to make won't be easy. We'll have to shift to new ways of using and making energy – but we have all the technology we need right now. We're good at finding new ways of doing things; we'll be OK.

The hardest thing will not be doing enough soon enough. That's an unknown cost, which could involve way more scary things than old pants.

Come on, *it's too late to stop climate chaos*, and anyway anything I can do is irrelevant, **isn't it?**

You say: I know how you feel,

but really it's not too late. The world will get warmer, but if we can keep temperature increases down to 2°C max, we will just stop things getting too bad. But that means acting now.

And the other thing is, you really do count – anything you do matters because then you are part of the solution, not part of the problem. The main thing is that if each of us acts, our government will have no excuse – it will have to make the cuts that are needed through new laws. So don't go floppy on me, we can do this.

 The back cover shows just how easy it can be

›› Step **10**

Reject the **ridiculous**

On occasion we are all ridiculous. But this step will help.

It works like this.

Next time you are about to buy something, simply ask yourself if your purchase of that crazy packaged-up beef burger is worth planetary chaos, mass starvation and general unpleasantness. Almost magically you will find you know the answer.

So, repeat after me. I do not need my oranges individually wrapped; I believe their existing skin to be adequate. I do not need to heat the outside of my house with a gas-fired patio heater; I am capable of going inside.

Easy eh? I think you have the idea. Let's move on.

OZONE UNFRIENDLY

NOW WITH EVEN MORE PACKAGING

AIR FREIGHTED FROM CALIFORNIA

+

FREE CARBON BOOST INCLUDED

100% NON RECYCLABLE

53

This good

*Good products
are well made,
save energy and
have a long life.*

solar power phone charger

wind-up radio

solar light

rechargeable batteries

dynamo torch

or buy nothing for a day?

This bad

*Bad products
are unnecessary
or are designed
for short, silly lives.*

---
gas-fired patio heaters
---
double cheese-burger in a box
---
lettuce from California
---
throw-away batteries
---
city living four-wheel drives

Tell us the best or the
maddest and baddest things
you can find – details to
icount.org.uk/stepbystep.

11
Look
good

Brace yourself – you will need your steely mood. You see, it's the car. If you don't own one – or never get in one – you're pretty special, and you can sit this one out. Otherwise, the carbon can needs dealing with.

Let's do it.

Your car is close, I know it. Let it see you. Walk towards it now. Rattle the keys, and, yes, that's right, run your finger along the paint. Yes – steady – now go like you're going to get in, and ... walk – well done, brilliant. Yes, keep going – break free. Breathe. Look at the sky. Notice stuff.

because ... I'd quite like less wobbly bits

When you get to where you need to be, you should feel chuffed. Every one of these short car journeys you miss saves around 2kg of carbon. And your body is already beginning to love you. It's that primeval hunter-gather feeling that laughs in the face of blubber.

Use a bike and you can expect to be as fit as someone 10 years younger. Try that nice charity **sustrans.org.uk** for more bike joy, and **cyclescheme.co.uk** for a tax-free bike for work.

5 things to do with love handles:

1 take your handles cycling
2 dance with them
3 take them to the shops
4 walk them to work
5 wobble them

Now, this is for your own benefit. Some habits kind of feel like they're good, but they aren't.

Flying, for instance.

There's no way round this. Aircraft just pipe greenhouse gases into our upper atmosphere, where they immediately do most damage.

Let's get this in perspective: fly to Athens and to make up for your climate impact you will have to go without heating, cooking, lighting and all forms of motorised transport for 2 years and 3 months. Which you don't really fancy, do you?

So you have to promise.

I hereby solemnly swear that:

I won't fly when I can take the train or boat.

I will take more holidays in my lovely, comfy UK.

I will use video conferencing technology.

I will take at least one less flight a year.

 Sign here please

If you're sure you really need a car, then make it a new hybrid version – you'll even get a grant of around £700.

Go to the Energy Savings Trust at est.org.uk to find out more. And 4x4s? Get one if you have lots of mud round your house, otherwise stop being so silly.

✂ *Here's a little something for your car*

My other car is my feet

Your next task is public transport – a remarkably useful invention. Here's something to keep you occupied.

Sudoku a: fiendishly difficult  *long journey*

7	4				1	2	8	
					6	4	9	
			4	8				
5	2					1		
	8			5			3	
		6					2	4
				4	9			
	5	1	8					
	9	8	3				1	2

To play – complete the grid so that every row, every column and every 3 by 3 box contains the numbers 1 to 9. Answers at icount.org/stepbystep

Sudoku b: easy *short journey*

9		4		3			2	
8				7	5	1		4
		9				7	6	3
	5		1	8				
	9	1				6	8	
				6	2		5	
5	3	7			4			
2		6	7	1				9
	1			2		3		8

By the way, no need to wrestle your entire week's shop onto the bus – get it delivered and save around 700kg of carbon a year.

 *You're getting there*

›› Step

Think

For this step, think.

Think forest. Think tree.

Along with oceans the world's forests might help to protect us from climate chaos – unless we continue to set light to them, or chop them up. Each year they absorb around 7 billion tonnes of carbon. Look at it like this – forests are the lungs of the world.

If you buy something made of wood – a good long-lasting material – look for a: which will mean it comes from a managed forest, and hasn't been ripped out of someone's ancestral land.

FSC

And bring trees into your life – you need your dreamy head for this. Start close to home.

Give a tree as a present. Plant one. Join a community woodland project. Stand still. Look up at the leaves. Consider that we stand to lose up to a third of all land-based species within our lifetimes. A large proportion of these critters and plants we won't even have a name for. Nice one.

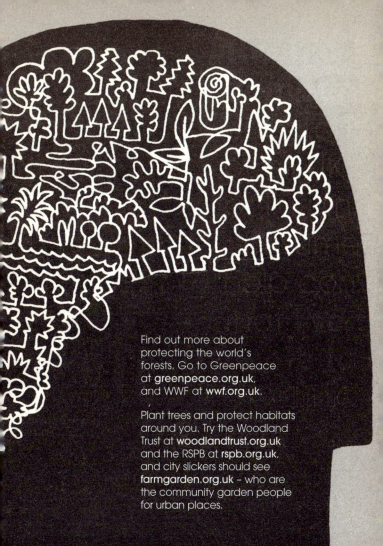

Find out more about
protecting the world's
forests. Go to Greenpeace
at **greenpeace.org.uk**,
and WWF at **wwf.org.uk**.

Plant trees and protect habitats
around you. Try the Woodland
Trust at **woodlandtrust.org.uk**
and the RSPB at **rspb.org.uk**,
and city slickers should see
farmgarden.org.uk – who are
the community garden people
for urban places.

I think ... I might
just go hug a tree

Drive your car 33 miles a day and you need at least 21 good-sized trees to absorb all your carbon for the year. Doesn't sound much, does it?

But if we wanted enough trees to cope with all our home-grown carbon pollution we would need to plant a new area of tropical forest more than 1.5 times the size of the entire UK.

It won't work. You can't plant trees to stop climate chaos. You have to save energy.

You, big foot

See the smallest footprints? These are the world's poorest people, who consume and have the least. When it comes to climate chaos these are the people with the smallest impact.

We, on the other hand, consume most of everything, and have very big footprints. But guess who's most at risk from climate chaos?

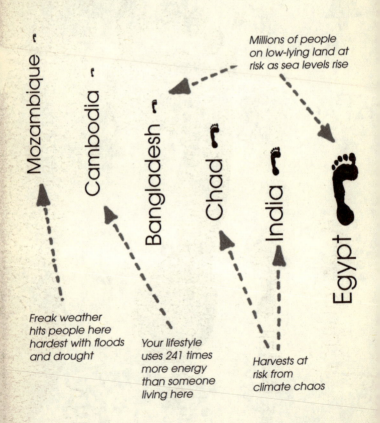

Mozambique

Cambodia

Bangladesh

Chad

India

Egypt

Millions of people on low-lying land at risk as sea levels rise

Freak weather hits people here hardest with floods and drought

Your lifestyle uses 241 times more energy than someone living here

Harvests at risk from climate chaos

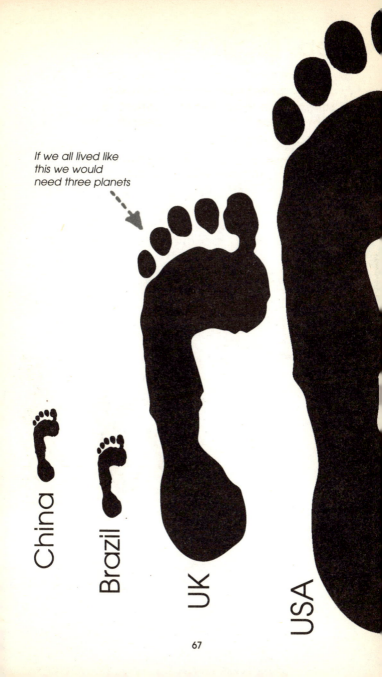

If we all lived like this we would need three planets

China

Brazil

UK

USA

67

Share stuff

Sharing is a kind of magic – it disappears things.
We've done the bath already, but it works in
all sorts of ways. Suddenly you have less of
everything. Two car journeys become one car
journey. Two mowers become one mower.
Two cars become one car. With numbers like
this, this step is highly recommended.

- **lift share** – car sharing for taking the kids to school saves 730kg of carbon a year

- **car share** – join a car sharing scheme

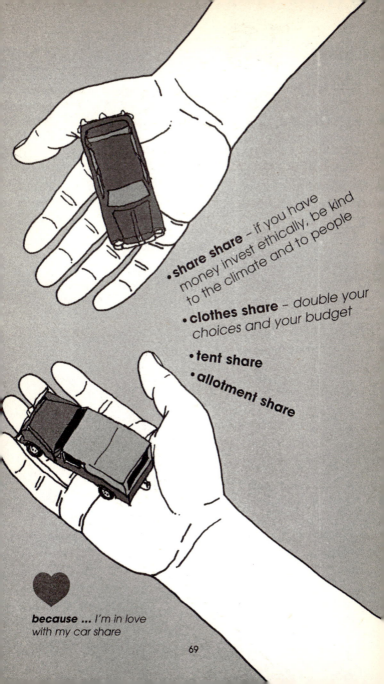

- **share share** – if you have money invest ethically, be kind to the climate and to people

- **clothes share** – double your choices and your budget

- **tent share**

- **allotment share**

because ... I'm in love with my car share

69

Never stop

This isn't over.
The trick now is to never stop dreaming.

Dream of forests and cool breezes and the flow of water. Dream of warm energy-efficient houses, of your own power from the sun, and a grant to buy a bike from your boss. Dream of the poorest people getting help with clean energy. Dream of solar water-heaters, of clean buses, and a council that actually comes and collects your recycling off you. Why not? Let yourself dream of the future.

This day is yours. Make it count.

dreaming

 **Dreams come true.** *Find out what's happening around the world, from intelligent houses in Denmark to solar power in India, go to icount.org.uk/stepbystep. The answers are out there.*

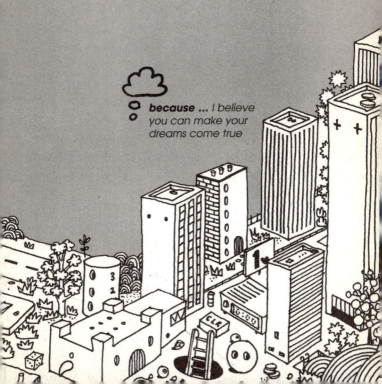

because ... I believe you can make your dreams come true

Dream your dreams

A few sounds to inspire your dreams...

Curtis Mayfield – 'Move On Up'
Primal Scream – 'Keep Your Dreams'
Bob Marley – 'Get Up, Stand Up'
Nina Simone – 'I Wish I Knew How It Would Feel To Be Free'
Sam Cooke – 'A Change Is Gonna Come'
The Coral – 'Pass it On'
Kanye West – 'Touch The Sky'
The Beach Boys – 'This Whole World'
The Flaming Lips – 'Race For The Prize'
The Arcade Fire – 'Wake Up'
The Impressions – 'People Get Ready'
Sly & the Family Stone – 'Everyday People'
Louis Armstrong – 'Wonderful World'
Talk Talk – 'Life's What You Make It'
Jimmy Cliff – 'You Can Get It If You Really Want'
Aaliyah – 'Try Again'
U2 – 'Walk On'

Add your songs at **icount.org.uk/stepbystep**

Share your dreams

on the windscreen

Oh dear

What a big 4x4 you have. How about a super-efficient hybrid next time?

We **can** stop climate chaos

at the office

Win £100!

An energy-saving bulb nets you around £100 in its long bright life. There's an idea.

We **can** stop climate chaos

on the bus

Hello beautiful bus person

Sitting here stops climate chaos – your trip on a bus creates way less carbon pollution than a car.

We **can** stop climate chaos

in the supermarket

Have you faced your carbon elephant?

Every glass bottle you recycle saves 0.5kg of carbon pollution.

We **can** stop climate chaos

73

Make noise, be visible

WE'RE STU
LEAVE PO
kind OF
ARE IN

Now you get to sit back. It's someone else's turn to carbon count – all you need do is lay down the challenge using your inbuilt voter power.
We are going to make some noise.

You see, the bottom line is that whatever you can do, the government can multiply it. Cleaner cars – it can make it law. Sharing clean technology with the world's poorest countries – it can see it happens. Better buildings that don't leak heat – it does it.

ED if WE TICS TO THE EOPLE THAT RESTED IN it

Prepare yourself for a little political action with this **Stretch, bend, ready?** *Let's go.*

First off, the facts.

If we're going to stop climate chaos, this is what the government has to do.

No nonsense – at least 3% year-on-year carbon reduction.

Take a lead – round the world the UK government has to work for agreement to cut carbon pollution. World-wide carbon pollution must be in decline by 2015.

Help the poorest countries get access to clean energy, help them cut out poverty and deal with the climate disasters they are already facing.